STRANGE BUT TRUE

Tiny Creatures

Timothy J. Bradley

Consultants

Timothy Rasinski, Ph.D.
Kent State University

Lori Oczkus
Literacy Consultant

Tejdeep Kochhar
High School Biology Teacher

Based on writing from
TIME For Kids. *TIME For Kids* and the *TIME
For Kids* logo are registered trademarks of
TIME Inc. Used under license.

Publishing Credits

Dona Herweck Rice, *Editor-in-Chief*
Lee Aucoin, *Creative Director*
Jamey Acosta, *Senior Editor*
Lexa Hoang, *Designer*
Stephanie Reid, *Photo Editor*
Rane Anderson, *Contributing Author*
Rachelle Cracchiolo, *M.S.Ed., Publisher*

Image Credits: cover, pp.1, 6, 7 (top), 8,
14–17,18 (top & bottom), 19 (middle), 21,
24 (top), 26–27 (top), 28–29, 38 (left), 39,
45 Photo Researchers, Inc. p.10–11, 22–23,
32–33, 35, 40–41 Timothy J. Bradley; pp.18
(left), 43 BigStock; p.8–9 Getty Images/
Flickr; pp.14, 30–31 iStockphoto; All other
images from Shutterstock.

Teacher Created Materials

5301 Oceanus Drive
Huntington Beach, CA 92649-1030
http://www.tcmpub.com
ISBN 978-1-4333-4862-4

Table of Contents

Little Lives

Enormous creatures like whales and lions get lots of attention. But there are billions of unseen creatures on our planet. Their numbers are large. And so are their effects!

Being tiny has its advantages. These creatures need fewer resources to survive and reproduce. Some of the tiniest creatures are the toughest. And they can survive conditions that would kill any human. Dive into this strange, invisible world, and find out just how tiny these tiny creatures can get!

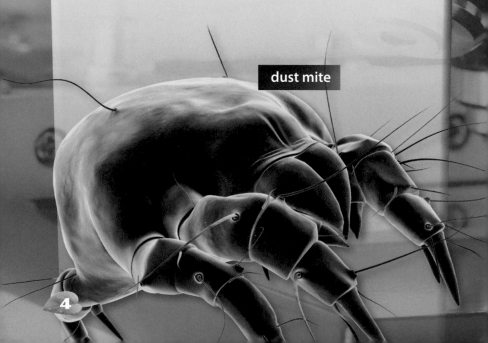

dust mite

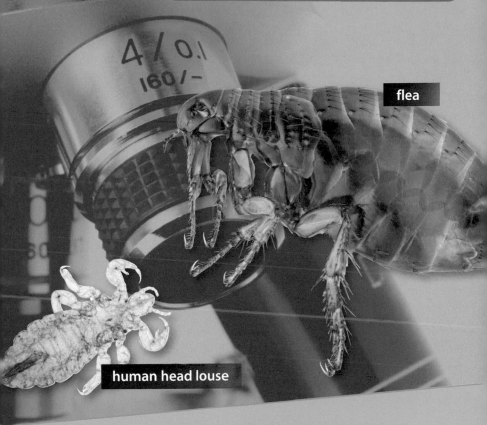

The images in this book have been magnified—BIG time! Some are shown at 100 times bigger than their natural size.

flea

human head louse

THINK LINK

1 What are the smallest creatures on Earth?

2 What are the advantages of being small?

3 Why are tiny creatures so important?

Bullet Ants

Bullet ants build their nests at the base of trees in the rainforest. These ants have the most painful sting in the world. Victims shake and moan as the ants' **venom** affects their muscles. The intense pain lasts for days.

Bullet ants aren't **aggressive** creatures. But they will defend their nest if it is disturbed. The worker bullet ants look for food in the top layers of the rainforest. They use their **potent** sting as a way to kill prey. Multiple stings from these little bugs can kill a human.

The stinger and venom are located at the back of the bullet ant's body.

Schmidt Pain Index

Scientist Justin Schmidt has been stung by more than 150 different types of insects! Based on his experience, he created a system to compare the stings of different insects. Take a look at how he ranks the sting of these nasty creatures in the Sting Pain Index.

4.0+ Bullet Ant

A sting in your toe will make you feel as if your whole foot is on fire. Avoid this mighty ant at all costs.

4.0 Tarantula Hawk Spider

It's about as bad as sticking your finger in an electrical socket.

3.0 Paper Wasp

This feels like acid on a papercut. Nasty!

2.0 Bald-faced Hornet

Experts say it feels like getting your hand stuck in a door.

1.0 Sweat Bee

Try pulling just one hair on your arm. It feels a bit like that.

Deadly Assassins

Like many spiders, the **assassin** spider is small but deadly. But it is different from other **arachnids** (uh-RAK-nidz). An assassin is a person who kills another person in a surprise attack. Most spiders prey on insects. But the assassin spider preys on other spiders. That's why they are called *assassins*!

The assassin spider was only just discovered. Scientists think there are hundreds of new spiders still to be found.

Discovery

Forty million years ago, a tiny spider crawled into a bubble of tree sap. Over time, the sap hardened and turned into amber. In the 1840s, a piece of amber was found with a fossil of an assassin spider in it. Before then, no one had seen a spider like this. Thirty years later, the first living assassin spider was found.

Ferocious Fangs

An assassin spider stabs its prey using the fangs at the end of its long jaws. Its long neck allows it to lift its massive mouth.

Assassin spiders can be found in Australia, Madagascar, and South Africa. There are 62 species of assassin spiders around the world.

The Assassin Strikes!

The assassin spider attacks its prey from afar. Its head, neck, and jaws are very long—the perfect length for striking!

1 The sly assassin sneaks up to another spider's web. It tugs on a strand and the web moves. The other spider is excited! It thinks an insect is caught in its web. Little does it know that the assassin is waiting.

2 The assassin waits for the perfect moment. When the other spider passes by, the assassin thrusts its sharp fangs into the victim's body.

3 The assassin lifts its victim off the ground. Deadly venom flows from its fangs into the other spider.

4 The assassin spider retracts its head and jaws. It's time to feast!

Ticks

These small **parasites** feed on blood. And most ticks get their blood from birds and mammals, including humans. Ticks cut open the skin. Then they feed on the victim's blood. The body of a tick can swell to be 200 to 600 times bigger after a large, bloody meal.

Ticks can spread diseases to humans and other animals. Ticks can even pass more than one disease to their **hosts**. Ticks are known for spreading Lyme disease and Rocky Mountain spotted fever.

Ancient Bloodsuckers

Scientists believe that ticks appeared on Earth long ago. Tick fossils have been found from the **Cretaceous Period**. The fossils date from 65.5 to 145.5 million years ago. At that time, dinosaurs ruled Earth.

Ticked Off

Here's the best way to remove a tick. (Make sure an adult is there to help.)

➢ Grab the tick's body near the head with a pair of tweezers.

➢ Pull it straight out.

➢ Go see a doctor!

Lice

Lice are tiny wingless insects. These parasites prey on birds and mammals, including humans. Many species of lice feed on the dead skin of their hosts. Other lice feed on blood. Like many parasites, lice can spread diseases to their hosts.

Lice are known for nesting in human hair. The little insects spread easily from person to person. The adult lice lay eggs. They use their saliva to attach the eggs to hair. When it dries, the saliva acts like a strong glue. As the lice bite, the host may have an itchy scalp. Special shampoos and lotions can kill the lice.

Making the Leap

Scientists believe that lice spread from gorillas to human ancestors about two million years ago.

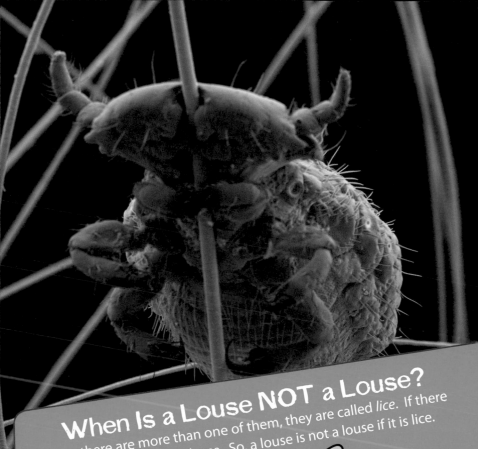

When Is a Louse NOT a Louse?

When there are more than one of them, they are called *lice*. If there is only one, it is called a *louse*. So, a louse is not a louse if it is lice.

Dash the dog was covered with lice.

After the vet shampooed him, there was only one louse left.

15

Fleas

Fleas have the ability to leap distances 200 times their own body length. They are one of the best jumpers in the insect world.

Fleas don't have wings. But they have mouths that are built for piercing skin. The body of a flea is flat and tough. Step on a flea and it will be just fine.

These pests breed very quickly. One mother flea can lead to hundreds of baby fleas. And they are all looking for blood. Fleas survive by biting their hosts and drinking the blood. Because they breed so quickly, fleas can become a big, itchy problem very quickly.

A female flea lays over 2,000 eggs in its lifetime. All it takes is one pregnant flea to infest an entire house!

Stop Scratching!

When a flea bites a human, it injects saliva into the bite. The saliva causes an allergic reaction, which makes the bite itch. Fleabites can be soothed with anti-itch cream. Try not to scratch!

Dig Deeper!

Deadly Pests

Even the smallest creatures have played a big role in human history. The **plague** is a nasty disease spread by fleas. It has caused more than 100 million deaths. Use the hot-spot colors to learn about history's largest outbreaks from this tiny pest.

Today

6th Century
The Mediterranean hosts the first recorded plague. It moves through major trade routes.

14th Century
By the end of the century, one third of Europeans are dead from plague.

17th Century
Another outbreak spreads from North Africa to Germany.

Sick Symptoms

If you have the plague, you'll know within days. Watch for these symptoms.

headaches	shivering	a strange feeling
fever	painful muscles	of happiness
vomiting		

14th

6th

18th

17th

19th

18th Century
Countries in the Middle East are plagued by disease.

19th Century
China is home to a plague that results in more than 10 million deaths.

Today
Modern antibiotics prevent outbreaks and make the plague less deadly.

Phorid Flies

These small flies are found throughout the world. Many species of the phorid (FOR-id) fly live in tropical regions. Others can be found around the house. In some places, they are known as *coffin flies*. The name comes from the dead flesh and decay the flies eat. Some of the food they eat carries harmful bacteria. Phorid flies are famous for spreading diseases.

These bugs are tiny. About as thin as a paper clip, they can be easy to miss. The life span of this little insect is also small. Phorid flies only live between 14 and 37 days.

Crime Solvers

Insects' close relationship to death and decay can be more than gross. It can be useful, too. Some insects, including phorid flies, help police figure out the time a person died.

1. When a person dies, the body starts to rot.

2. Flies and other insects feed and lay eggs on dead bodies.

3. Police find the dead body and look at the insects and eggs covering it.

4. **Forensic entomologists** study the insects and their life cycles.

5. The age of the insects helps experts figure out whether the body has been dead for a couple of days or several weeks.

DIG DEEPER!

Off with Their Heads!

Some types of phorid flies are known as ant-**decapitation** (dih-KAP-i-tey-shun) flies. Can you guess why they were given that name? The story of the ant-decapitation fly begins with the female who is looking for the perfect place to lay her eggs.

1 The female flies gather at the entrance to an ant nest.

2 As the ants pass by, the flies insert eggs in the ants' bodies.

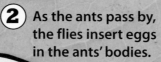

3 The eggs hatch inside the ants and move into their heads.

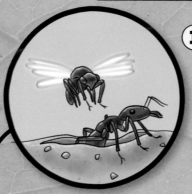

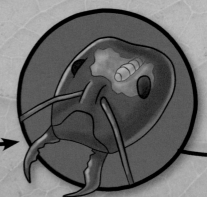

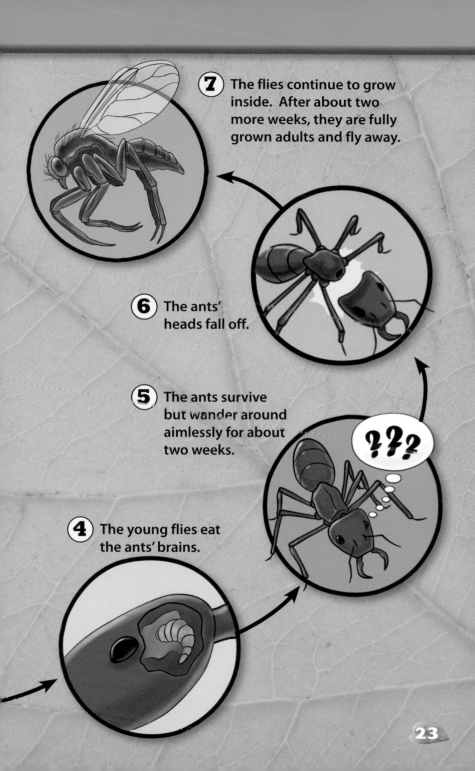

7 The flies continue to grow inside. After about two more weeks, they are fully grown adults and fly away.

6 The ants' heads fall off.

5 The ants survive but wander around aimlessly for about two weeks.

4 The young flies eat the ants' brains.

Micro Critters

Microorganisms are tiny creatures. Some are smaller than a strand of hair. Often, they can only be seen with a magnifying lens or a microscope. The term *micro* means "very small," so it's a perfect word to describe the small critters in this chapter.

These tiny creatures cover a big area. They live nearly everywhere on Earth. They are found in water, soil, and hot vents deep on the ocean floor. They can even be found high in the Earth's atmosphere.

Although microorganisms are small, it doesn't mean that they aren't important. Scientists around the world have spent their lives studying these micro creatures. Because of their research, biologists know that some micro creatures live alone. But some live in colonies. Some of them eat living things. Others are a good source of food themselves. Most importantly, researchers know these small creatures can have a big impact on humans.

bacteria magnified

microorganisms grown
from a human sneeze

Measuring Up

Micro means "one millionth." That's $\frac{1}{1,000,000}$! A
micrometer is one millionth of a meter. There are
1,000,000 micrometers in a meter.

Nematodes

Worms come in all shapes and sizes. The nematode (NEM-uh-tohd) is a type of worm. Some species are invisible to the naked eye. A microscope is required to see them. They may be small, but they are fascinating. These worms can wiggle between grains of sand. They can also live in the toughest **habitats**, nearly one mile underground. They have even survived a space shuttle explosion! Many of them are parasites. They can cause diseases in humans, animals, and plants. Nematodes make up 90 percent of the organisms that live on the ocean floor.

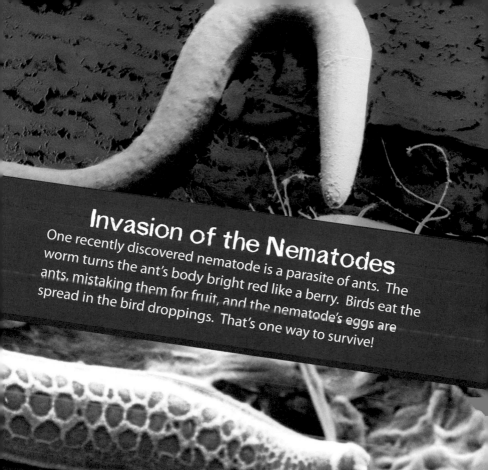

Invasion of the Nematodes

One recently discovered nematode is a parasite of ants. The worm turns the ant's body bright red like a berry. Birds eat the ants, mistaking them for fruit, and the nematode's eggs are spread in the bird droppings. That's one way to survive!

Going Deep

Nematodes have been found as far as 3,000 feet below ground.

Tardigrades

These little creatures can be found in almost every habitat on Earth. Tardigrades (TAHR-di-greydz) have been found in the highest mountains and deep in the sea. They survive on frozen ice caps and in hot tropical waters. Lakes and ponds are one of their favorite habitats. Mosses and lichens are also places they like to live. Most tardigrades are plant eaters. But some species are predators.

They are very small. But tardigrades are about the toughest creatures on Earth. They can survive 10 years without water. Tardigrades have even traveled into outer space! They survived eight days in the **vacuum** and extreme cold of space. They can take the high pressures of the deepest seas. Even temperatures of 300°F won't kill them.

Tardigrades have stubby bodies and four pairs of legs. They look like miniature caterpillars. The name *tardigrade* means "slow walker."

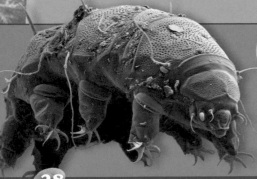

Living Fossils

Tardigrade fossils have been found in rock that is about 500 million years old!

When tardigrades were first observed under the microscope, they were named *water bears* because of their shape and the way they moved.

Tough Bugs

In harsh environments, the tardigrade can bring its **metabolism** to a complete halt. Some can live like that up to 120 years! And once the tough conditions improve, the tardigrade returns to normal.

Nano Creatures

Nano creatures are everywhere. They live in the soil we walk on and the water we drink. They are even in the air we breathe. They live *on* our bodies and *in* our bodies.

The Greek term *nano* means "extremely small." But scientists are learning big things from these little ones. **Nanotechnology** is a new field of science. Experts study the tiniest creatures to learn how they survive. They are able to live in unusual places. They travel through the tightest spaces. With more research, they hope to build nano robots. These machines will be able to work inside the human body or deep inside huge space ships. It's a big job for tiny technology—inspired by the world's tiniest creatures!

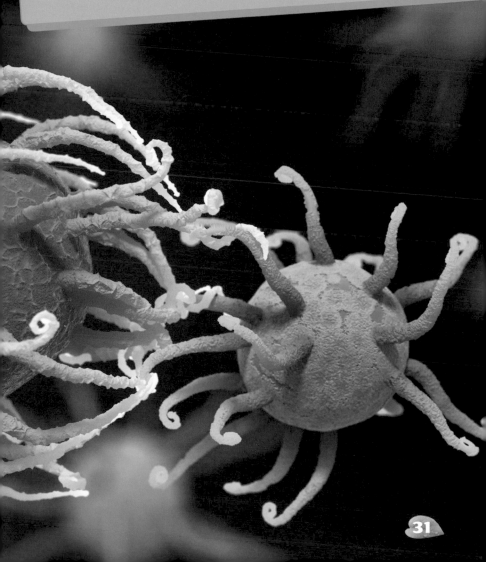

Nano Power

A nanometer is one billionth of a meter. That's $\frac{1}{1,000,000,000}$! That means there are 1,000,000,000 nanometers in a meter. As far as we know, only atoms and molecules are this size. No creature is actually this small, but the smallest microscopic creatures deserve their own special word!

Going, Going, Gone!

The world is filled with tiny creatures. When you're talking about such measurements, it's good to keep them in perspective. Take a look at how these creatures measure up.

human

bullet ants

about 2 meters tall
m = meter
about 3 feet

2 centimeters
the size of a thumb
centimeter = $\frac{1}{100}$ meter

10 micrometers

$\frac{1}{10}$ the width of a human hair

1 micrometer $= \frac{1}{1,000,000}$ **meter**

plankton

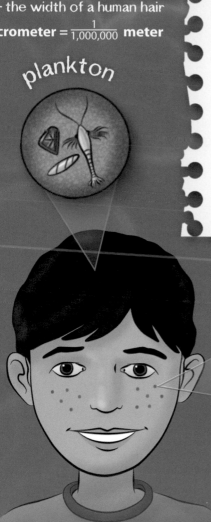

STOP! THINK...

- What are the advantages of using different units to describe these tiny animals?

- Why do you think it took people so long to discover these tiny creatures?

- How can we study such small life forms?

phorid flies

2 millimeters

the size of a freckle

1 millimeter $= \frac{1}{1,000}$ **meter**

Plankton

Plankton are tiny organisms that live in the ocean. Phytoplankton are tiny plants. They use **photosynthesis** to make their food. Phytoplankton live near the surface of the ocean where there is a lot of light. Zooplankton are tiny animals that drift in the ocean. Some of these animals stay small all their lives. Others will grow to be fish, sea urchins, or starfish. There are many ocean conditions that can affect plankton. Plankton must go where the current takes them. And they never know what they will find. Ocean pollution is one danger. Plankton are an important source for the fish that feed on them. If the plankton are in danger, thousands of fish are in danger, too.

Big Predators, Tiny Prey

Some of the largest creatures in the ocean feed on the smallest. Whales, like the baleen whale and the blue whale, can eat hundreds of pounds of microscopic plankton per day!

An Ocean of Life

Tiny organisms like plankton are the first link in the food chain of the ocean. Plankton feeds many creatures, large and small.

zooplankton

phytoplankton

mackerel

Plankton feeds many creatures, large and small.

shark

tuna

Dust Mites

These little **arthropods** have adapted to living with humans. The stable world inside a house is perfect for them. Dust mites feed on flakes of dead skin left behind by humans. They don't live on humans or animals, but they can be found in furniture, bedding, and carpet.

Small body parts and remains from the mites can cause serious allergies in humans. Dust mites can even cause **asthma** in some people. Asthma is a condition that causes the air passages in the lungs to swell up. The lungs aren't able to take in enough air to support the body.

Washing and cleaning furniture and clothes can lower the number of dust mites. Experts advise that freezing pillows and toys can kill dust mites. A carpet-free house also makes it much easier to avoid mites. But every home has some dust mites—no matter how often it is cleaned!

People who suffer from asthma may use an inhaler to ease symptoms.

Mighty Thirsty

To survive, dust mites absorb moisture from the air and store it in the sides of their heads. When they get thirsty, they can suck the water into their mouths. In extremely dry seasons, mites gather together and share water.

Under the Microscope

If these organisms are so small, how do we know they are there? We need a microscope to see them. There's even a special kind of microscope that takes very close pictures of these small creatures. The **scanning electron microscope** can see down from the micro level all the way to the nano level!

dust mite

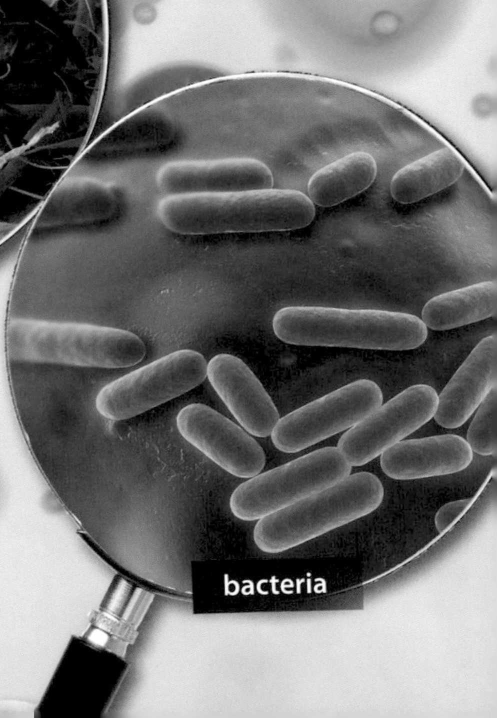

bacteria

Taking photographs through a microscope is called *photomicrography.*

flea

plankton

A First Look

The invention of the microscope has changed the world. Just a few hundred years ago, people had no idea these organisms existed. Antonie van Leeuwenhoek (LAY-ven-hook) was the first to observe microorganisms through the microscrope. Today, scientists are able to study these creatures in detail.

The Big Finish

Our planet is nearly 8,000 miles in diameter. It is home to billions of creatures and millions of tiny mysterious worlds. With mighty microscopes and careful study, we are learning about some of the most amazing critters on Earth. They can cause a massive plague or feed an enormous whale. They can slip into the smallest corners of the world or fill an entire ocean. They can strike like a deadly assassin or hide in an invisible world. Whether they are living in our hair or deep underground, these tiny creatures have some big effects. And they have much to teach us about surviving in this wild world.

streptococcus

bacillus

E. coli

41

Glossary

aggressive—ready to attack

arachnids—arthropods such as spiders, scorpions, and ticks

arthropods—animals with segmented bodies, jointed limbs, and a shell

assassin—someone who kills an important person

asthma—a condition that causes the air passages in the lungs to swell up

Cretaceous Period—a time in Earth's history 145.5 to 65.5 million years ago

decapitation—the act of cutting the head off an organism

forensic entomologists—people who study insect biology and how it applies to crimes

habitats—where organisms live

hosts—organisms that have a parasite living on or in them

metabolism—the process in which cells break down or build up substances essential for life

nanotechnology—the art of using and controlling materials on a very small scale, particularly on the atomic or molecular scale

parasites—organisms that live on or in host organisms

photosynthesis—the process by which plants make energy from water and air in sunlight

plague—a disease, spread by fleas, that may kill many people
potent—powerful
scanning electron microscope—an instrument used to study objects at the atomic level
vacuum—a space without matter or air
venom—a toxic substance

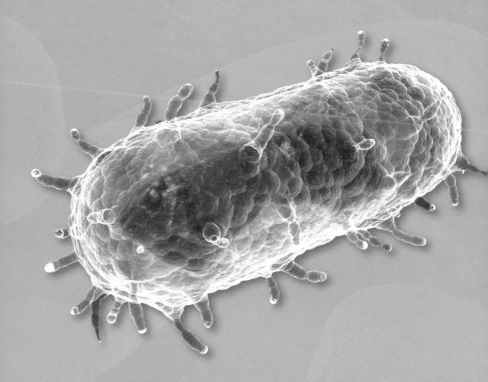

Index

Bibliography

Jackson, Donna M. *The Bug Scientists.* **Houghton Mifflin Books for Children, 2002.**

Following several scientists, this book takes a look at bugs that crawl, swim, and jump. Settings include the morgue, an outdoor classroom, and a bug festival with a cricket-spitting contest and cockroach races.

Snedden, Robert. *Yuck! A Big Book of Little Horrors.* **Simon & Schuster Children's Publishing, 1996.**

Huge color photographs show a magnified view of common household items and the tiny creatures that lurk in every corner.

Walker, Richard. *Kingfisher Knowledge: Microscopic Life.* **Kingfisher, 2004.**

This book examines how some organisms help us fight diseases and produce food, but others can be harmful, causing tooth decay, food poisoning, and deadly epidemics.

Zamosky, Lisa. *Investigating Simple Organisms.* **Teacher Created Materials, 2008.**

Find out more about Antonie van Leeuwenhoek's microscopic discovery and how scientists classify the smallest plants and animals.

More to Explore

The Bug Club
http://www.amentsoc.org/bug-club

This website is for anyone interested in insects and creepy crawlies.
There are several sections, including games, insect identification tips, and
Bug Club for schools.

Burge Pest Control
http://www.burgepest.com

This pest control website has excellent photos of the pests you might find
around your home. Experts show you how to tell the difference between
ants, termites, wasps, bees, spiders, roaches, bedbugs, fleas, ticks, and
silverfish.

Get This Bug Off of Me!
http://www.uky.edu/Ag/Entomology/ythfacts/stories/hurtrnot.htm

This website has photos and descriptions of bugs that aren't harmful,
including daddy-long-legs, millipedes, and cockroaches. The bottom of
the page lists bugs that can bite or sting, such as centipedes, scorpions,
and fleas.

Monsters Inside Me
http://animal.discovery.com/videos/monsters-inside-me-videos/

This series of short videos briefly describes 17 different parasites, whom
they affect, and the damage they leave behind. These dynamic videos are
sure to make you squirm.

About the Author

Timothy J. Bradley grew up near Boston, Massachusetts, and spent every spare minute drawing the biggest dinosaurs to the tiniest creatures. That was so much fun that he started writing and illustrating books about natural history and science fiction. Timothy also worked as a toy designer for Hasbro, Inc., and designed life-size dinosaurs for museum exhibits. After writing this book, he had nightmares about thousands of microorganisms crawling under his skin. Timothy lives in sunny Southern California with his wife and son.

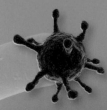